CW01460676

LIFE TRAPS

Avoid these life traps and live in Peace

M. Vincent Alexander, M.D.

Xulon PRESS

Introduction

For many years, I have periodically pondered many situations and decisions that I might have handled differently. Another way of looking at it is if I could live the situation over again (e.g. if I were reincarnated although I don't believe such a thing) what and how would I live that situation over again given a new set of choices. But beyond that I have analyzed a set of challenges God set before men that offer pleasures and if misused, long term penalties ranging from embarrassment to loss of peace, to death.

Although the book of James in the Bible says God does not tempt man, I contend that God set up pleasures for mankind that are full of loaded "traps" and the worst thing about these pleasures is that they explore the weakest parts of man's integrity...his instincts and his emotions and this is the reason I wrote this book of warnings.

I will be quoting the Bible frequently. Bible quotations are taken from the King James Translation unless otherwise specified.

Overview

God's own word issues warnings in most of these areas that are potential traps but there are two problems with the effectiveness of the warnings in God's word:

1. It does not go into emphatic "down to earth detail"
2. Very few people read the Bible (God's Word) carefully paying strict attention and discerning details in life situations and even fewer are

skillful in applying God's Word to life's fluid situations.

Man has been frequently caught in the same traps ever since he has been on the Earth. Avoiding these 6 traps can make life so much easier. These traps are:

1. The Mouth
   a. Mindless talking, thoughtless speech, useless uninspiring talk
   b. Mindless and thoughtless eating and drinking
   c. Unwise or illegal indulgence of/ in alcohol or drugs
2. Coveting
   a. Failing to *control* the desire to have (the desire for food evokes aggressive territorial instincts that can be lethal)

b. trying to dominate other men or women (this desire to control other people is disobedient and disrespectful to God and I will show this in scripture later in this book)

3. Sex

   a. Allowing sex (the act) or eros (sexual love) to dominate one's Life and purpose which is as dangerous as a loaded gun or "armed" land mine. (Interaction between men and women that is not well thought out is as unstable as nitroglycerin and just as deadly as a rattlesnake.)

   b. Anger erupting between the two sexes over small carnal things can be quite poisonous.

4. Unforgivingness
   Unforgivingness can land you in hell for sure. There are only 2 sins the Bible says that cannot be forgiven:
   a. Blaspheming the Holy Spirit
   b. Unforgivingness–an important scripture passage Mark 11:23-27 has Jesus speaking "Whosever shall say unto this mountain, *be thou removed and cast into the sea and shall not doubt in his heart, but believeth that what-soever he sayeth shall come to pass, he shall have whatsoever he sayeth, therefore whatsoever ye desire when ye pray, believe that ye shall receive it and ye shall have it.* ***And when ye stand praying, forgive for if ye do not forgive***

men of their trespasses, neither will your heavenly father forgive you of your trespasses. Not only will your prayer go unanswered, but should you die before you have opportunity to forgive this person(s), then you will die not being forgiven by your heavenly father. The stain of unforgivingness will chase you right into hell. You will not be allowed in heaven with a heart carrying unforgivingness. This is a clever trap engineered by self righteousness.

5. Anger (mismanaged anger)
   a. Persistent anger linked to self righteousness is the lethal com-

panion of unforgivingness and is a trap.

b. Unmanaged persistent anger can rob you of eternity with God in peace and is a wide open door to hell.

6. Pride

a. Pride is an imposter or impersonator of righteousness

b. It is a clever deceiver and is a deadly killer and will "mess you up" permanently if you are not careful. In the book of Proverbs in the Holy Bible, God warns through the inspired writer "Pride goeth before the fall".

In the following pages in this book I will expand on these 6 life traps. Some descriptions may be instantly clear, others not so clear, and some may be edgy and possibly some at first thought offensive but at second thought straightforward. I sincerely hope that avoiding the 6 traps I discuss will keep you and/or your family or friends ***out of trouble not only here on Earth but also in elementary spiritual matters as well*** with just 2-3 hours of reading.

Life Traps or Pleasures, Beware !

The first pleasure or trap I wish to discuss takes us back to the Garden of Eden. It is the mouth gate. That first pleasure leads to the first statement.

CLOSE YOUR MOUTH. If you close your mouth, a gate to hell is closed. Stop doing the Devil's bidding. The Devil enticed Eve by way of food. Food enters the mouth. Eating is a powerful natural instinct. Although Eve was not starving at all, nevertheless, this powerful instinct allowed her to be seduced in conversation with Satan and to question her known boundaries, and eventually eat of a forbidden fruit. Once her instinct was exploited enough she was no match for the wiles of the devil and she was soundly beaten. This caused the first step of separation from God and when she gave the fruit to Adam he was no match for the seduction of the food instinct (fruit) and no match for the seduction by Eve (his wife, if you will) whose seduction was now even more than "eros" but with increased power by Satanic inoculation. (Note: Adam apparently had no direct conversation with Satan). Nevertheless, Adam ate of the forbidden fruit at the suggestion of his wife, Eve.

Now we have already established that the mouth and desire to eat can open the gate of Hell and through the underlying vice of GREED.

Let's take another view. The mouth can open the gate of Hell by talking or speaking. Jesus is quoted in Matthew 12:34-37 saying, (v.34) " O generation of vipers, how can ye being evil speak good things ? for out of the abundance of the heart, the mouth speaketh .(v.35) A good man out of the treasure of his heart bringeth forth good things: and an evil man out of the evil treasure bringeth forth evil things.(v.36) But I say unto you, That every idle word that men shall speak , they shall give account thereof in the day of judgement.(v.37) For by thy words thou shalt be justified and by thy words thou shalt be condemned ". In Proverbs chapter 18 verse 21, it says "Death and Life are in the power of the tongue and they that love it shall eat the fruit thereof ". James 3:8-10 tells us, "out of the same mouth proceeds blessing and cursing, then how is it that blessing and cursing comes from the same mouth. These things ought not to be." In James 1:19, it says, "let every man be swift to hear, slow to speak, slow to wrath". In James 4:10-12 it says, " Humble yourselves in the sight of the Lord and He shall lift you up. *Speak* not evil one to another brethren. He that speaketh evil of his brother and judgeth his brother speaketh evil of the law and judgeth the law, but if thou jud-geth the law, thou art not a doer of the law, but a judge. There is one lawgiver who is able to save and destroy: who art thou who judgest another ?" All of the above quoted scriptures describe functions of the mouth and of speech. I'd like to point out at this time that the word Satan translates as *gossiper, accuser and slanderer.* The above scriptures clearly warn against gossiping, accusing and slandering, if you think about it. Jesus in John 10:10 declared, " The thief (*the devil*) cometh not, but for to steal, and to kill, and to destroy: I am come that they might have life and that they might have it more abundantly. People have become experts at stealing, killing and destroying with their mouths. ***These are TRAPS of the mouth. Gossiping, accusing and slandering can land a person in hell,*** since they are now doing the Devil's work for him with their mouths through speaking. Men have become progressively looser with their mouth and lips speaking things in public forums that should only be spoken in private. People are saying things on social media such as Twitter and Facebook, that should only be spoken face to face or in private. I have been astonished by things spoken Congressional members, and even by ministers and preachers disrespectfully and ***publically*** criticizing even those who should be recognized as colleagues or allies and not even taking time to get all the facts and circumstances understood. One disturbing example of a U.S. House of Representatives Congressional member yielding to Satan's work occurred Sept. 10, 2009, when a South Carolina Congressman (Rep. J.W.), called President Obama a liar when the President said illegal aliens would not be covered by the Affordable Care Act. He screamed the word "liar" on National television bringing disorder and indignity to a previously orderly and nationally televised public meeting without even having any of the facts. (The Affordable Care Act had not been finished.) I witnessed this on a national television network and found this incident on the CNN internet display as well. ***I do commend the Congressman for later calling the White House directly and apologizing for his outburst also noted on the CNN website.*** This is the reason we must be careful before we speak. A particularly disturbing example of clergy attacking clergy comes to mind when a televangelist whom I previously admired for many years for his encyclopedic Biblical knowledge called Pope Francis corrupt and a false prophet without any facts or proof. Pope Francis has proven himself to be a dear, kind, and loving man. Pope Francis has even begun to oversee bridging some very wide gaps between the Catholic Church and the Protestant churches working with the Lutheran denomination. According to scripture, the evangelist I speak of should seek to speak one on one with the Pope before spreading venom over national T.V. Jesus outlined the proper way to do this. One conveniently forgotten scripture by *so called or self called Christians* is Matthew 18: 15-17 (v.15) "Moreover, if thy brother shall trespass against thee, go and tell him his fault between thee and him alone: if he shall hear thee, thou hast gained thy brother. (v.16) But if he will not hear thee, then take with thee one or two more that in the mouth of two or three witnesses every word may be established. (v.17) And if he neglect to hear them, tell it to the church, but if he neglect to hear to hear the church, let him be unto thee as a heathen man and a publican".(KJV)

Notice this biblical passage ***does not say***, if you have a disagreement; first take it to Twitter or Facebook, then to NBC, ABC, CBS, Fox, and then to MSNBC, Fox News, CNN, or ESPN.

I heard things spoken *not to* but about the elected President of the United States,

Barack Obama on television and in the printed press, at the State of the Union messages that are insulting, cowardly and racist, and totally undignified. Not once did I hear one of these critics say I am personally going to speak to the President about this issue or that issue. Not once did they bring an issue directly to the President. No, they took it to Social Media, print media and the television networks, ***first.***

If Christians ignore the instructions in scripture, small wonder that the secular world pays no attention to scripture.

The President has been accused of being a Muslim when he said he was a Christian. (I have known some Muslims who were clearly people of integrity) The President professes he is a Christian.

Who are these people who think they are as omniscient as Jehovah God such that they can decide who is a Christian or not ? I would love to test them and see if they can quote the Word of God they claim to believe and do they practice the Word of God out of Love for God is Love. Well, these ACCUSERS ARE NOT Jehovah God nor do they represent Jehovah God nor the Lord Jesus Christ. They actually represent Satan by doing Satan's work. Remember one translation for Satan is ***ACCUSER.*** Best case scenarios, these accusers are ***lousy ambassadors for Christ.*** Galations 6:1 says " If a man be overtaken in a fault, let him who is spiritual restore such a one in a spirit of meekness (humility), considering thyself lest thou also be tempted. The word

Satan also translates as "Gossiper" as well as "Accuser". Does not the Outline of "the Law", THE TEN COMMANDMENTS say " Thou shalt not bear false witness". Does not Jesus warn that one should confront a contending brother face to face (recall and remember Matthew 18:15-17). Does not the book of Ephesians confirm that "man shall be judged by every idle word he speaks". I assure you that if what is spoken is not a quote of the word of God, it is probably idle. Not every good word spoken will be a direct quote from the Bible. But in ordinary conversation in any given day, a good way to test the word is by this mnemonic I learned from my pastor 2 years ago. Before speaking run it through the think filter and ask yourself, is it ?:

T- Thoughtful

H-Helpful

I – Inspiring

N- Necessary

K- Kind

This THINK nmemonic was given by Dr. Steven L. Lowery in a sermon exhorting his congregation at the National Church of God in Fort Washington, Maryland as a guide to help keep conversations as godly as possible.

If what you are going to say truly meets these criteria with Jesus as the judge, then say it; it's OK. If not, think again.

People, even professing Christians, have left off to be wise and do God's word. They think they can say any irresponsible, insensitive thing because it is 1st Amendment guaranteed right or is politically expedient or cute or gathers a crowd and say these things even slanderous things (another translation of the word "SATAN" is " SLANDERER") lying without remorse. They do this without remorse (even professing Christians) because they have done it so much that their consciences are seared as if with a hot iron or poker. having allowed their hearts or even their spirits to be branded by the chief accuser, gossiper, and slanderer, SATAN. These people lie calling themselves Christians and not really knowing what the word CHRISTIAN means.

CHRISTIAN = CHRIST + IAN
Christ = Anointed One IAN = little
Christian = "little anointed one"
or "one with little anointing"

An anointed person:

1. Lays hands on the sick and the sick recover from the illness

2. Ministers or preaches the Good News Gospel of Jesus Christ into all the world

3. Is fearless: if they drink any deadly thing they are not hurt

4. They operate in the 9 gifts of the Spirit as needed

5. Instead of speaking public accusations and criticism they speak in tongues.

6. They exhibit the 9 fruits of the Spirit diligently, consistently, with honest commitment.

Now if you are anointed and manifest the list of 6 criteria listed above or are working on that list daily, then call yourself a Christian disciple. If not, hold your peace. You have not done your homework and you are a POOR AMBASSADOR OF CHRIST.

Some people manifest the 9 fruits of the Spirit without the gifts.

If they are consistent with the fruit, and minister or preach the Good News Gospel of Jesus Christ to every creature, then they are already Excellent Ambassadors of Christ.

Five of the most evil uses of the mouth in the area of speech on a large scale are:

1. The News Media
2. Politics
3. Sales of products and services
4. Preaching on giving and receiving especially tithes and offerings

insincerely and deceptively (money can be a deceptive trap even for those with good intentions)
5. The Internet

The News Media and Politics I have already addressed to some extent before.

In sales of products and services, people and companies and even large corporations have sold products they knew did not work, were overpriced, dangerous, and useless and hid these facts from the public and from local, state and national governments or from organizations they supposedly were servicing. This is nothing more than lying. " All liars shall have their part in the lake which burneth with fire and brimstone"(Revelations 21:8). Jesus referred to the "Lake of Fire" where the worm dieth not and the fire is not quenched in Mark's Gospel chapter 9 verses 44, 46, and 48.

Too often preaching on tithes and offerings, giving and receiving in some churches and ministries are out of context, offending both man and God. It can be a blessing or a trap. Cain (Abel's brother) found that truth out. Jealousy entered into giving and "worshiping God" and turned a potentially *good act* into a murder, in fact, the first recorded murder. This was worship through giving poisoned by a bad attitude. God forbid. The love of money is the root of all evil. Of course as one of my beloved teachers taught, "Ministries operate on grit, grace and greenbacks". That is reality. TITHING is more complicated than just 10% of the gross. Thought needs to go into giving/tithing. Tithing off the net is safer and can keep one out of jail. Some businesses have high incomes but have very high overheads. If a business owner tithes off of the gross of that business, he or she may not make the payroll for their employees, may not be able to pay taxes in accordance with the law, and may wind up in jail and with no business and no credibility.

Example:

A certain business grossing $ 1,000,000.00 has many employees and a lot of equipment such that after expenses and paying payroll what is left is $ 120,000.00. If one tithes 1/10 off the gross, the tithe will be $ 100,000.00.

The operator of this business will have $ 20,000.00 left over. This person will place his family in poverty in less than one month. He will surely lose his family if he is the only income source. Notice I did not mention insurance, liability insurance, or other business expenses or even taxes or quarterly tax estimates which businesses must file. They have to be paid as well. In some cases a proprietor may miss paying his payroll to employees if he did not take it out in advance and tithed it before fulfilling the payroll obligation to his employees who also may have families. ***If you are sure you can tithe off the gross, do it and be blessed accordingly, but don't get into bondage in so doing. God loves a cheerful giver. In my church, the pas-***

tor's ask "which part of your income do you want to be blessed". I think this is a great way to look at it, and there is no pressure or coercion here in this statement, just encouragement.

Let's get real. Money is evil. Money is addicting. Stop and think. Suppose we tithed chickens or corn or tomatoes or broccoli or fish caught in the stream or bay. What would our churches do with these bountiful offerings? Would they graciously receive our chickens or fish or reject them. How would they quantify these precious gifts? Money is "man made" and is a man made trap. The Lord said "you cannot serve God and Mammon". YOU JUST CAN'T DO THAT.

The weightier matters of the Gospel are:

1. Justice
2. Mercy
3. Love (Charity)
4. Forgiveness

These weightier matters deserve our attention first of all.

There are nine gifts of the Spirit and nine Fruits of the Spirit:

We who claim to be Christians need to operate in the nine gifts of the Spirit as needed, but we are REQUIRED to operate in the nine Fruits of the Spirit in order to "begin" to be an effective "Ambassador" of our Lord and Saviour Jesus Christ. The nine gifts of the Spirit operate only through love. That means that nine gifts of the Spirit which are:

1. Word of Wisdom

2. Word of Knowledge
3. Faith (special faith)
4. Gifts of Healings
5. Working of Miracles
6. Prophecy
7. Discerning of spirits
8. Divers kinds of tongues
9. Interpretation of tongues

operate only through love or by the nine fruits of the Spirit:

1. Love
2. Joy
3. Peace
4. Longsuffering
5. Gentleness
6. Goodness
7. Faith
8. Meekness

9. Temperance (self-control)

sufficiently for effective operation of the Spiritual gifts. With the evil in our nation, it is no small wonder that Spiritual gifts in the last 16 years, since 2000, seem so hollow and inconsistent. Some people operate the nine Fruits of the Spirit without the nine Gifts of the Spirit quite well. They are also great Ambassadors for Christ and honor the Lord well.

The Internet deserves special mention. Although it requires no mechanical movement of the mouth, it is incredibly dangerous and is a way of talking, trapping, and "phishing". Phishing is an internet trick of putting out what appears to be an official message with an implied fear of consequences message if not replied to with personal information attached in a complete manner. The original message is neither true nor official but can succeed in coercing a person/victim in giving up vital personal information in the reply ultimately leading to attempted "identity theft". As mentioned before, social media is a venomous snake when used by evil people. I already mentioned People are saying things on social media,Twitter, Facebook, etc. that should only be spoken face to face or in private. As I said before, I have been astonished by things spoken in Congress, and even by ministers and preachers disrespect- fully ***publically*** criticizing even those who should be recognized as colleagues or allies and not even taking time to get all the facts and circumstances understood. Again, a conveniently forgotten scripture by *so called or self called Christians* is Matthew 18: 15-17 (v.15) "Moreover, if thy brother shall trespass against thee, go and tell him his fault between thee and him alone: if he shall hear thee, thou hast gained thy brother. (v.16) But if he will not hear thee, then take with thee one or two more that in the mouth of two or three witnesses every word may be established. (v.17) And if he neglect to hear them, tell it to the church, but if he neglect to hear to hear the church, let him be unto thee as a heathen man and a publican".(KJV). Again, notice this biblical passage ***does not say***, if you have a disagreement; first take it to Twitter or Facebook, then to other media. I can't turn this loose, but I heard things spoken *not to* but about the elected President of the United States, Barack Obama on Social Media that are insulting, cowardly and racist, and totally undignified. Not once did I hear one of these critics say I am personally going to speak to the President about this issue or that issue. Not once did they bring an issue directly to the President. No, they took it to Social Media, print media and the television networks, ***first.***

If Christians ignore the instructions in scripture, small wonder that the secular world pays no attention to scripture.

The Internet's Social Media has components which can land you ***in hell for sure. Twitter and Facebook are notable examples. Man shall be judged for every idle word he speaks. If he is***

not speaking the word of God, it is idle.
If that is a problem for you, ***"TOUGH".***

There was a time when the News Media Organizations prided themselves in accurate and balanced reporting. Now the goal is sensational and hyped up reporting which goal is to accuse and spew out as much venom propaganda in as short a period of time as possible. If news agencies were telling the truth without bias then you should be able to change to other channels news programs and get agreement in the stories much like the four gospels agree with each other. They agree and yet are different. They agree first of all in spirit. Once there is spiritual agreement, the details soon agree.

Politics is consumed with criticizing the "opponent" or the opponent's political party. Criticism without helping or destructive criticism is surely the Devil's work. Much too often I hear politicians say they have the answer to this problem or that problem. But they never want to share the solution as part of a team, but always seek to make themselves appear superior to their opponent and superior to everybody else. They even say they know more than experienced experts. In fact they inadvertently claim to know more than God. They often say "trust me". They never say trust God. They have never heard of II Chronicles 7:14. That scripture says, "If my people which are called by my name shall humble themselves and pray and seek my face, and turn from their wicked ways; then will I hear from heaven and will forgive their sin and will heal their land ". Neither have they heard the scripture I Timothy 2:1-5 which says, "I exhort therefore, that, first of all, supplications, prayers, intercessions, and giving of thanks, be made for all men; for kings, and for all that are in authority; that we may lead a quiet and peaceable life in all godliness and honesty. For this is good and acceptable in the sight of God our Saviour; Who will have all men to be saved, and to come unto the knowledge of the truth. For there is one God and one mediator between God and man, the man Christ Jesus."

If God should bless America these politicians would learn of the scripture II Timothy 3:1-5. "(v.1) This know also, that in the last days perilous times shall come. (v.2) For men shall be lovers of their own selves, covetous, boasters, proud, blasphemers, disobedient to parents, unthankful, unholy; (v.3) Without natural affection, trucebreakers, false accusers, incontinent, fierce, despisers of those that are good. (v.4) Traitors, heady, highminded, lovers of pleasures more than lovers of God; (v.5) Having a form of godliness but denying the power thereof; from such turn away". ***Having a form of godliness, but denying the power thereof; FROM SUCH TURN AWAY".*** No group fills these deceptively evil traits more than self serving politicians.

Proverbs 17: 27-28 says (v.27)"He that hath knowledge spareth his words: and a man of understanding is of an excellent spirit.(v.28) Even a fool when he holdeth his peace is counted wise: and he that shutteth his lips is esteemed a man of understanding".

A person who talks on a cell phone while driving is distracted and dangerous. A pedestrian crossing the street talking on a cell phone is careless and is putting his or her life at risk needlessly. Scripture tells us "God takes no pleasure in fools".

Appetites other than food exist. Food deserves a discussion as a potential trap, but other oral appetites are as dangerous or more dangerous such as:

1. Drugs
    a. Prescription...
    b. non prescription...
2. alcohol

a. whiskey
b. beer
c. wine
d. mixtures of the above

3. Tobacco
   Nearly all tobacco products contain addicting substances such as nicotine. Manipulation of tobacco by men have made these products ***highly*** addicting.

   A word to the wise is "leave them alone". Help is available in various forms if you are already trapped.

Coveting – ***uncontrolled desire to have*** is a dangerous and potentially fatal trap.

" As a general rule, man's a fool, if it's hot he wants it cool; if it's cool he

wants it hot, he always wants what he ain't got. "The above is a quote from *my* pastor's grandfather. It is so perfectly down to earth and yet so true and so spiritual if you actually think about it. (Man-forever double minded, not good).

A. Wanting more than what you need:
1. Food
2. Cars
3. Household items
4. Land
B. Lust
1. For power and influence
2. For money
a. Evading taxes legally
1. No laws broken but failing to or being unwilling to assist in one's own community for school improve-

ments such as for textbooks, computers, athletic fields, athletic equipment, trash disposal, health facilities, police and fire, general services and etc. because it raises taxes by one hundred dollars per year or less while failing to consider the welfare of society as a whole.

b. Evading taxes illegally
   1. Failing to file
   2. Frankly cheating on taxes

3. Sex
   a. Fornication
   b. Adultery
   c. Jealousy

C. LACK of COMPASSION is often a manifestation of COVETOUSNESS when there is disregard of:
1. The poor
2. Fatherless
3. Widow
4. Elderly
5. Retired
6. Disabled
7. Veterans
8. Homeless
9. ***The responsibilities of CAPITALISM. Capitalism without compassion is not an expression of Freedom, it is simply COVETOUSNESS.***

Coveting or covetousness can also be thought of as an uncontrolled desire to have or dominate. In nature, among animal creatures, we see territoriality well demonstrated. When a predator takes down a prey or other creature for food to eat, it is not uncommon to see other species go after *the kill.*

Hyenas and buzzards are examples. We even see it among the same species such as male lions competing for dominance of a certain "pride" and fighting nearly to the death or to the death for dominance. The loser is expelled in either case and the winner gets to mate with all the females in the pride. The cubs who are offspring of the "loser" male are mercilessly killed by the "winning" male immediately apparently eliminating the DNA of the loser out of the pride and stopping any nursing activity which prevents pregnancy in the adult female lions in the pride. I suspect that this instinct is what drives certain types of covetousness. Unquestionably, this instinct to dominate families, communities, nations, and even churches is present even in humans. In humans the fights are usually not physical but verbal, subtle, and clandestinely clever. Money is usually involved. Greed is often involved.

Wanting more than what you need is not the way taught to us by Jesus, the Christ. Wanting that which doesn't make sense just to have it or just because you can have it and someone else can't is coveting. Wanting that which belongs to someone else is coveting.

Wanting to acquire a fortune at someone else's or some other group's expense so that they don't or can't acquire their fortune is coveting.

Acquiring a fortune and then working to increase that fortune while others assets decrease proportionately is coveting. Capitalism without discipline is large scale coveting. This driving instinct amazingly is seen in lions, rhinos (rhinoceros species) and hippos (hippopotami). But humans are supposed to be reasonable. Real Christians should live above this instinct consistently or at least hopefully. "If your eye (vision probably being the main sense for covetousness) offends thee, pluck it out and throw it away ".

A few examples of covetousness are worthy because they have teaching value:

1. Food (shows up again as a trap in another area)–People see food at

smorgasbords and attempt to eat all they can eat all that they can get into their stomachs. People in supermarkets garner up as many of one item as they can. They may get a lower price "buying in bulk". But in the long run this practice can increase demand and raise the price for everybody (Economics 101). This cause inflation. It also causes those with less wealth to then use up the buying power that they have less efficiently.

2. Some people walk right into ownership or leasing cars they really can't afford. They see someone else with an attractive expensive vehicle or are lured by vanity filled advertising into purchasing an auto they really

can't afford. Soon their life is out of balance and that fancy auto becomes an albatross around their neck.

3. Some people are lured by clever advertising to buy houses or even household items ranging from cookware to kitchen appliances to furniture. Sometimes the cookware and appliances never get used and the furniture just becomes clutter. Moderation is key in purchases. Even the wealthy need to exercise moderation in purchases. It really is a societal responsibility.

Lust (coveting on steroids) takes various forms. Selective forms of lust include:

1. Lust for power – "control freaks", having to be in control.

Inability to share control of marriage, businesses, churches, government, and finances is characteristic of such individuals. They "have to be" in charge. They pursue titles which identify them being officially in charge, but rarely help anyone because they are much too busy pleasing themselves.

2. Lust for money – lust for money makes a person disregard their neighbor because these people feel they should own all goods and services and land. The state or government should own nothing. Other people should own nothing. These people are unable to understand the concept of commonwealth or common shared interest. When

a community is truly a community of concerned citizens honestly pursuing the well being of all of the citizens in the community they become a commonwealth. The state of Virginia actually officially calls itself the "Commonwealth of Virginia". A commonwealth of earnestly concerned citizens doesn't mind at all being taxed for good reasons e.g. textbooks and computers for schools, first rate athletic fields, courts and tracks, recreation and learning centers, and libraries. They don't mind being taxed for needed general services, such as trash collection, police and fire coverage, ambulance and hospital services. Payment for these services are generously understood and not unfairly avoided. On a national level, funding for Armed Forces is accepted with a spirit of unity. Veterans and their activities are well funded or should be. If a spirit of covetousness prevails in a community or nation, veterans are honored with speeches, but when it comes to helping them financially recover after they have put their lives at risk or have been uprooted in a mobilization for war or conflict or humanitarian service, no one steps forward as a cheerful giver. This is silent covetousness and PHONY concern. Phony concern and this type of clandestine covetousness are twins. Failure to demonstrate compassion to veterans, the fatherless, widows, the elderly, the retired, the disabled, the homeless is a form of passive covetousness.

3. Lust for land – Lust for land is a type of covetousness that seems to cloud many people's judgement. Real Estate developers seem to be highly susceptible to this form of covetousness. Such people want to own all the land they can get control of even if it hurts someone else. They often want to have their names on buildings. They will not hesitate to hurt someone else in order to get what they want. They avoid paying fair price for land exchanges. They will claim land that is not theirs if

they get the chance. They will claim mineral rites on land that they have sold at fair market price. This is covetousness for land. They fail to recognize the sovereign ownership of God of all things on planet Earth. The scripture Exodus 19:5-6 says, " Now therefore if ye shall obey my voice indeed and keep my covenant, then ye shall be a peculiar treasure unto me above all people ***FOR ALL THE EARTH IS MINE*** and ye shall be unto me a kingdom of priests and a holy nation. This ye shall speak unto the children of Israel." Despite people claiming, a certain property is theirs, God effectively says Uh,Uh, "ALL THE EARTH IS MINE." The final proof is that no person has ever taken any land with him when he or she died (or dies).

Although the above mentioned lusts have been around for hundreds and even thousands of years, only since the advent of modern day computers have these forms of lust mentioned above become so dangerously out of control and a threat to humanity in general. BEWARE. This gate to hell is wide open.

Sexual Lust will be handled as the major topic *SEX*

SEX

A New Jersey pastor who pastored in the Trenton area in the early 1960's once was quoted in a sermon saying

"Everyone cross your legs. Now the gates of hell are closed". STOP THINKING ABOUT SEX WITH LUST IN MIND.

This could be interpreted as dry, cold and insensitive.

I have lived 68 years and I interpret this as true but unfortunately sex is not the only open gate to hell. We have already mentioned several ways to go to hell already. Sex is a powerful trap. It is too strong and to convoluted for even bears to break out of. Worse yet, evil and ulterior motives are hidden in it like the most devastating of land mines, IED's, and have a pull and a draw like magnetic ship mines and once sex traps snags a person, it is as difficult to get away from as a pressure sensitive land mine. Sometimes the sex trap is inescapable without the direct intervention from Jehovah God in order to escape the trap and it's devastations, , fornication, marital turmoil, failed marriage, adultery, strife, and etc. No wonder that the 1960's pastor from New Jersey recommended to his congregation (metaphorically, I guess) that "everyone cross their legs, the gates of hell are now closed". I am not sure we have to go that far literally, but outside the context of God ordained marriage, sex should be dismissed from our minds. And even within marriage, sex is seasonal, at best. There is a time for embracing and a time not to embrace. There is a time and place and season for everything under heaven. This must be understood even in marriage. If it is not understood, pain and confusion, and disappointment in marriage is just around the corner. Instead of sex, think on these things listed in Philippians 4:8. Whatsoever things are true, whatsoever things are honest, whatsoever things are just, whatsoever things are pure, whatsoever things are lovely, whatsoever things are of good report; if there be any virtue, if there be any praise, think on these things. Only Jesus has all of these characteristics. Stop thinking about sex. Think about Jesus, the Christ.

"Eros" or physical (erotic) love is probably the lowest form of love. It is certainly short lived, usually. Eros is hormonally driven. Probably, it's best feature is it helps to some extent to propagate the human species.

I have occasionally asked the Lord why he chose meiosis for humans and certain other species as a means of reproduction. Some living species reproduce by mitosis in which mature cells divide and produce an identical copy through an elegant division of the cell nucleus in a specific phase and an equal division of the cells cytoplasm. The copy cells eventually grow to maturity and then they themselves divide and so on. Some species can be hermaphrodites and are male and female within the same individual and create unique reproductive options. Mitosis is the method of choice for one cell organisms and a few multicellular organisms. Interestingly, the cells of our skin, gastrointestinal, and respiratory tracts reproduce by mitosis lifelong. This is true in humans, other mammals, birds, reptiles, amphibians (frogs and salamanders) crustaceans and fish. Although Amphibians use meiosis for reproductive specie propagation, they can change gender or have two genders in the same individual, if necessary to accomplish specie reproduction. You may ask why I am going into this with this degree of detail ? Because I believe the Lord God had options. I suspect He was allowing His creatures another method of expression of love or agreement. But this, of course, carried certain risks, and if misused, or abused, tragic and painful consequences ensue.

A word about the spiritual aspects of sex is only fair. Hebrews 9:22 states " And almost all things are by the law purged with blood; and without the shedding of blood is no remission"(of sin). When a female is a virgin and the hymen is broken during coitus, a circumferential bleeding occurs for a short period. This establishes one point of the cleansing bloodshed. Circumcision which is a circumferential cut of the redundant foreskin of the penis accomplishes a second point of the cleansing bloodshed through which the male seed or sperm passes during sexual intercourse. Blood is shed in the male and the male and the female in sexual intercourse with a virgin and is spiritually and indefinitely maintained if the monogamous relationship is continued. This allows for remission of sin or cleansing in the sex act and cleansing in the potential reproduction and subsequent childbirth once the conceived child is ready to be born. "Without the shedding of blood there is no remission of sin(s) ". You see there is a bloodline in operation here. There is a cleansing here. But along with this there is obvious significant risk(s) since these events are hormonally driven in young males and females and "eros" is powerful both as friend or foe. Eros wants what it wants and considers the consequences later. Four warnings I leave with you:

1. Consider sexual/romantic love, "eros", as a possible enemy as well as friend.
2. Consider marriage with the utmost of care.
3. Don't ever lose "sight" of Jesus.

4. Fornication and adultery violate the sanctity and cleansing afforded by the bloodline corruptly and obviously. Think about it. But even these infractions can be cleansed in the dominion of Jesus , the Christ.

One subject needs discussion with sensitivity and frankness. That subject is *homosexuality.* Homosexuality is condemned in the Bible. Read Romans Chapter 1 versus 22-32. The passage speaks of man in his arrogance and pride refused to glorify God. Instead of being wise they became fools with vain imaginations. God then gave them over to their unclean lusts to dishonor their own bodies. And then picking up in verses 26 and going on to verse 32 I shall quote, (v.26)" For this cause God gave them up to vile affections: for even their women did change the natural use into that which is against nature: (v.27)And likewise also the men, leaving the natural use of the woman, burned in their lust one to another, men with men, working that which is unseemly, and receiving in themselves that recompence of their error which was meet.(v.28) And even as they did not like to retain God in *their* knowledge,God gave them over to a reprobate mind, to do those things which are not convenient. (v.29) Being filled with all unrighteousness, fornication, wickedness, covetousness, full of envy, , murder, debate, deceit, malignity, whisperers (*gossipers*). Verses 30 and 31 expand on the numerous unrighteous behaviors. If you practice homosexuality, you are playing Russian roulette(gambling) with your salvation. Can you still get into heaven ? YES, if you stop and request forgiveness and repent.

Only two (2) sins cannot be forgiven:

1. Blaspheming the Holy Spirit- stubbornly and unyieldingly denying the ministry and works of the Holy Spirit (Holy Ghost) whether you understand or not

2. Unforgiveness – Read Mark 11:25-26 (v.25) "And when ye stand praying, forgive, if ye have ought against any: that your Father; also which is in heaven may forgive your trespasses. (v.26) But if ye do not forgive, neither will your Father

which is in heaven forgive you of your trespasses".

If you die with unforgivingness in your heart, your destination is hell. What a shame that shall be because the other person probably wronged you but you took the bait when you're ordered to take no offense and hold it, but rather to forgive.

Personally, I think sexless civil unions are probably "OK". I refer the reader to I Samuel, Chapter 20 with special attention to verses 16 and 17. These men of God were committed to each other in a righteous wholesome way. Scripture tells us that their souls were knitted together. This is worthy of high level and sophisticated thought.

But if you like keeping things reflexively very simple, remember the New Jersey pastor, "Cross your legs, the gates of Hell are now closed ".

Now if you find yourself where you should not be, don't completely despair. The good news is we are given an escape(s) from our sin(s) in scripture:

1. Old Testament – Isaiah 55:6-7

Seek ye the Lord while he may be found, call ye upon him while he is near. Let the wicked forsake His way and the unrighteous man his thoughts, and let him return unto the Lord and he will have mercy upon him and to our God for he will abundantly pardon.

2. New Testament

I John 1:9 – If we confess our sins he is faithful and just to forgive us our sins and cleanse from all unrighteousness

If you have escaped from the clutches of corrupt eros, don't go back. Be strong. Be smart.

Galatians 5:1 Standfast therefore in the liberty wherewith Christ has made us free, *(you free)*, and be not entangled again with the yoke of bondage.

4. Eliminate Unforgivingness

Unforgivingness was discussed previously as part of another subject.

1. Mark 11:25-26 says, (v.25) "And when ye stand praying, forgive, if ye have ought against any: that your Father; also which is

in heaven may forgive your trespasses. (v.26) But if ye do not forgive, neither will your Father which is in heaven forgive you of your trespasses.

Unforgivingness is toxic. See the next section on mismanaged anger. Ephesians 4:26-27 warns "Be ye angry, and sin not; let not the sun go down upon your wrath. Neither give place to the devil. Ephesians 4:29-30 notes, "Let no corrupt communication proceed out of your mouth, but that which is good to use of edifying that it may minister grace unto the hearers. And grieve not the Holy Spirit of God whereby ye are sealed unto the day of redemption". Ephesians 4: 31-32

Finishes this subject with "Let all bitterness and wrath and anger and clamour , and evil speaking be put away from you with all malice, and be ye kind to one another even as God for Christ's sake hath forgiven you. "

5. Mismanaged Anger: the Evil Twin of Unforgivingness TOSS THEM BOTH OUT OF YOUR LIFE and be happier and live your appointed time! Proverbs 22:24 says have nothing to do with an angry man (or woman – no one gets a free pass here). The King James translation says "make no friendship with and angry man, and with a furious man thou shalt not go. "

Colossians 3:8-10 says, "But now ye also put off all these; anger, wrath, malice, blasphemy, filthy communication out of your mouth. Lie not one to another seeing that ye have put off the old man with his deeds; And have put on the new *man*, which is renewed in knowledge after the image of him who created him.

James 1: 19-20 says "Wherefore my beloved brethren, let every man be swift to hear, slow to speak and slow to wrath; for the wrath of man worketh not the righteousness of God."

Matthew 5:22 says, " But I say unto you, whosoever is angry with his brother without a cause shall be in danger of the judgement, and whosoever shall say unto his brother, Raca, shall be in danger of the council, but whosoever shall say, Thou fool shall be in danger of hell fire.

Anger will rob you of your eternity at peace with God. Persistent anger is the tag along lethal companion of the poison, ***unforgivngness.*** Persistent anger will sooner or later kill the bearer of the anger. Similarly, persistent anger is not just the instigator of suicide, but is the master of homicide. Anger may have a legitimate reason for existing among human relationships at all levels of endeavor, but God has warned in numerous times, events, places, and circumstances to dispose of anger quickly.

It causes relationship blindness to all concerned. It is the source of racism, sexism, green eyed jealousy, prejudices of all types, destruction and failure in all human endeavors. God has warned, "Be ye angry, *and* sin not: let not the sun go down upon your wrath. Neither give place to the devil." (Ephesians 4:26-27). I am so impressed that the scripture says, "Be ye angry AND sin not. Anger at a moment is certainly understood, since it is an emotion. That is why a conjunction *AND* occurs in verse 26 i.e. be angry (go ahead), but in that anger DO NOT SIN. Do not hold on to it and take no hostile actions nor say destructive things. Pray through it and rise above it. Do not sin. What are the sins to not allow to go forth from your being ? Put off from yourself all these: anger, wrath blasphemy, filthy communications, lying to one another, fornications, adultery, murders, assaults, slander, accusations, backbiting with the tongue(talking about someone behind their back or in social media), unforgivingness, holding grudges, vowing to never forgive someone, ambushes, bullying, extortion, blackmail, stealing, robbery, price gouging, using corrupt standards or weights, The foregoing is a list of the common sins in human endeavors and interactions.

Even if wronged, a person who is spiritually wise or truly godly will avoid the above sins if at all possible. A truly spiritually wise or godly person avoids taking offense. He or she recognizes Satan's bait in various situations and avoids it and surely will not take the bait. Persistent anger will trigger in the bearer:

1. Arthritis
2. High blood pressure
3. Diabetes
4. Relapse of nervous disorders such as MS, ALS and other motor neuron diseases
5. Weight gain
6. Weight loss
7. Myalgias

8. Possibly some types of Migraine

9. Exacerbation of allergies.

10. Sin

Be ye angry and sin not. Don't keep the anger and damage yours or somebody else's salvation for eternity.

6. Pride (unreasonable conceit)
Proverbs 16:18 says, "Pride goeth before destruction and an haughty spirit before a fall. "

OK, so ***pride goeth before a fall or before the fall. <u>Pride is the first deadly sin.</u>*** It got Lucifer thrown out of heaven (he really had a great fall just like the familiar story of Humpty Dumpty). Never think of yourself more highly than you ought. Scripture tells us that "the

Lord is the lifter of your head". God loves you but in Acts 10:34 scripture tells us, "God is no respecter of persons". This is confirmed in Romans 2:11. God thinks good thoughts toward you. In Jeremiah 29:11 God says "For I know the thoughts I think toward you, not for evil, but for good, to give you a future and an expected end", but he hates a haughty or proud look.

We are told in Psalm 146 verse 9 that the way of the wicked (which includes the prideful), the Lord will turn upside down.

My advice to the reader is to keep pride and "personal honor" in check. If you don't, the consequences will be unpleasant and if you are prideful too long, it will kill you not only in this life, but also in eternity. And being human, if you feel prideful, avoid saying it. Be reasonable. Jesus said in Matthew 6:31 actually in teaching on anxiety for worldly needs "Therefore take no thought saying". Being human, thoughts may enter our minds, but be careful about reciting those thoughts out loud where Satan may then take them to accuse us.

A special warning regarding pride is appropriate, especially in these times. Pride is sneaky. I did not call it a pleasure, but it is the first deadly sin. Man did not commit pride at first, because Lucifer did. It got him kicked out of heaven for all eternity.

I would not call it a pleasure, but it gives a false feeling of well being and inflated self worth. In the end, it does not please God.

Summary

We have covered a lot of ground. We need to summarize our discussions into useful plans of action.

1. CLOSE YOUR MOUTH
   a. Think before you speak
   a. Control your appetites
2. Stop Coveting
   a. Stop lusting – "cross your legs"
   b. Don't worship Mammon (money and influence)

3. Sexual Lust – avoid it like poison – dismiss it
4. Eliminate Unforgivingness
5. Get anger under control
6. Be wary of pride

If you deal with these 6 principle warnings successfully, you will surely avoid much pain and sorrow and you will get along with man well and most of all you will remain available for use by God 24/7/365. You will also be at peace with God. Furthermore, if you have not publicly received salvation through accepting the Lord Jesus Christ; you will be ready when that invitation comes and it will be an easy transition with no extra baggage. God bless you and may you have good fortune and favor. Good fortune and good luck are close, but good fortune is clearly under God's management. Good luck is mostly, but not entirely, under man's management. Either way, very best wishes in life from me to you. **Close off the gates of hell and then stand fast in the liberty wherewith Christ (the anointed one) has made you free and be not entangled again with the yolk of bondage.**

The Good News

I f you are already trapped already by one of the " pleasure traps ", accept Jesus as Saviour and Lord and be saved, delivered and set free.

Romans 3:23 says "for all have sinned and come short of the glory of God.

Romans 6:23 says "for the wages of sin is death, but the gift of God is eternal life through Jesus Christ our Lord.

Romans 10: 8-10 says "The word is nigh thee, the word of FAITH which we preach, that if thou shalt confess with thy mouth, the Lord Jesus (that he is the Son of God) and believe in thy heart that God raised him from the dead, thou shalt be saved, for with the heart man believeth unto righteousness and with the mouth confession is made unto salvation.

Romans 12: 1-2 says There is therefore now no condemnation to them that are in Christ Jesus who do not walk after the flesh, but after the Spirit, for the law of the Spirit of Life in Christ has made us free from the law of Sin and Death.

Receive the Gift of God which is eternal life through Jesus Christ our Lord when the invitation comes. Get ready! It's at the door.

Milton Keynes UK
Ingram Content Group UK Ltd.
UKHW010718180823
427095UK00001B/1